CW00571263

My Pet Revealed Jesus To Me

A Devotional and Reflective Journal

Dr. LaRhonda Perry-Howell and Dr. Siegfried Howell

About the Authors

Dr. LaRhonda Perry-Howell is an educator with over 25 years in education teaching elementary school students. She is married to Siegfried Howell, and together they have two adult children. Her love for her children brought her fear of dogs full circle as she allowed a puppy into the family. Through this process, LaRhonda developed a love for Xander and a stronger love for God.

Dr. Siegfried Howell has spent his life studying and perfecting his craft as an educator. He has over 24 years of teaching experience in elementary, middle, and high school science. He is an accomplished educator and author of many educational books designed for elementary and high school students. He never thought that his wife LaRhonda, and his new dog Xander would jump-start his relationship with God.

Copyright 2020 Dr. Siegfried and Dr. LaRhonda Perry-Howell

All rights reserved. No part of this publication may be reproduced or transmitted in any form or by any means, electronic or mechanical, including photocopy, recording, or any information storage and retrieval system, without permission in writing from the author.

Request for permission to make copies of any part of this work should be emailed to:

Dr. Siegfried E. Howell
DrSiegfriedHowell@gmail.com

DEDICATION

We wish to dedicate this book to our daughter, son, and pet dog Xander. Their zest for life and excitement has inspired us to write this book. Xander has allowed us to view life from his perspective as we learn to love God more. We pray that the stories found in this book bring you to a better understanding of God and His love for us.

Special Dedication

Special thanks to my dad Everette Howell and sister Richelle Howell for always giving advice and editing the books that I have written.

Table of Contents

Fear Over Love

When I was nine years old, I loved riding my bike everywhere with my sister. We would ride in the neighborhood, to the park, and in the woods near where we lived. One day while riding our bikes, my sister thought it would be a great idea to scare me for fun, so she screamed out, "Dog! Dog!" I took off riding as fast as I could.

My fear of being bitten was so intense. I didn't even take the time to see if there was a dog or where it was. I rode as fast and as hard as I could through the woods until I hit what I would later find out was a large mound of dirt. After my front tire went over the bump, I flew through the air before landing with a loud thump. My sister witnessed the whole thing and came to my rescue. By this point, she was sad and remorseful to see me on the ground, bleeding and dirty.

Until that day, I didn't know I had such an intense fear of dogs. After all, we had a dog at home. As my sister helped me up and towards home, I couldn't help but wonder why I reacted in such a panicked state. Maybe it was the tone of my sister's voice. But from that day on, I feared dogs. I wouldn't let a dog get close to me, not even for my kids who wanted one so badly; the fear was too great.

When my daughter was nine years old, my worse fears were remembered when she asked for a puppy. Although it was 23 years later, my fear for dogs seemed stronger than my love for my daughter. It would take another seven years for me to face my fear of dogs and allow a dog into our family.

In Genesis chapter 3, the story is told of the day Adam and Eve ate the fruit and sinned against God. The same day they sinned, God came searching for them in the garden, but they hid from Him because they were naked, ashamed, and fearful. From that day on, God did everything to show His unchanging love for man. The love of God was so very strong that it would overcome the fear of man to reveal the perfect love of God.

Reflection

Describe a personal situation when you displayed fear over love. What was the outcome of your actions?

_____

_____

_____

_____

_____

_____

_____

_____

_____

_____

Read the text found in Isaiah 35:4. Describe what God is willing to do for those who belong to him?

_____

_____

_____

_____

_____

_____

_____

_____

_____

_____

Love Over Fear

My daughter, Elandya begged for a puppy for over 18 years, but she never got her puppy. She did get, however, a brother she loved more than life itself. After 16 years with her beloved brother, she moved into her own place, an hour away, in a different city. Her brother missed her very much and one day, she came to us with her self-determined revelation.

While visiting us one weekend, our daughter sat me down and informed me that her brother had a hole in his heart from missing her. You see, about six months after she moved out, the COVID-19 pandemic spread through our state and closed everything down in our city. In one weekend, my son went from seeing his friends daily to communicating and living his whole life online.

She observed that her brother was very lonely and thought that his loneliness could cause him to spiral exponentially downward if he did not get something like a dog that he could develop a bond and a real relationship with. How could I not listen to this plea of help for our son? I would have to face my fear and entertain getting a dog if I wanted to save my son from a potential emotional spiral. I called my husband, and we discussed what was said and how we could adjust to having a dog in the family.

My fear was real and many questions and situations needed to be addressed for me to face them properly. This was the first time in five years that a legitimate argument was posed for me to throw my fears to the wind. I loved my daughter, and I loved my son, so I was now willing to do whatever was necessary to save my son from any unnecessary mental hurt or anguish. What had seemed impossible for me to embrace was now thought for me to consider actively. The love that I had for my son was strong enough for me to face my fear of dogs.

In Matthew 26, Jesus was grappling with taking on all the sins of the world. He felt the weight of sin and evil on His shoulders in the Garden of Gethsemane. He was fearful of what would come next, so He prayed to His Father, "Father, remove this cup from Me. However, not My will, but Thine be done." At that moment, the love He had for humankind far superseded the fear of being the Lamb of God. God sent His son, Jesus, as a sacrificial lamb for the sins of the world. Lambs are known to be helpless and vulnerable animals that must be guided and taken care of. For God to send His son as a sacrificial lamb, He showed His love for us over the fear of losing Him.

Reflection

Read the text found in 1 John 4:18. What does this text explain about perfect love and fear?

_____

_____

_____

_____

_____

_____

_____

_____

_____

_____

Are there current or past situations that you would respond to differently if you felt that you possessed the perfect love spoken about in the text above?

_____

_____

_____

_____

_____

_____

_____

_____

_____

_____

God Always Has a Plan

After I decided that I would try and allow my son to have a dog at home, a few things needed to be addressed. Everyone in the house and family had asthma. What would that mean for us? As educators, our first task came naturally to us; we educated ourselves. Everyone had homework to do. We all had a week to gather a list of safe dogs for a family with allergies and asthma.

After one week of research, we had a list of dogs considered safe for people with allergies and asthma. For our second task, we had to decide on the breed of dog that best fit the needs of our family. At the top of the list were Labradoodles (a mix between a Labrador retriever and a Poodle), Golden-doodles (a mix between a golden retriever and a poodle), and an Aussie-doodle (a mix between an Australian shepherd and a Poodle).

Deciding the size dog for our family was our third task. I, still fearful of dogs, wanted a dog that was as small as possible. Our son, however, wanted a dog that he could play with, snuggle up with, and run with. He was also very particular about the color; he wanted a golden colored dog. This left us with the Golden-doodle being the dog that was chosen for us. After picking the type of dog we wanted, the next task was to decide where we would get it and how long the wait would have to be. The further the location and longer the wait, the more time I had to prepare myself for the inevitable.

By this time, we were entering the summer days of June. My son was very excited, and my daughter, who was using her own money to buy her brother a dog, was ready to purchase the dog. Every weekend she came home to research different sizes of doodles, their prices, their availability, and their locations. This meant that every week, I had to deal with the reality that this family would own a dog sooner or later.

After weeks of research and phone calls to dog shelters, breeders, and online platforms, we settled on a breeder and a location. We now had to face the news that our puppy would not be available until October (the fall). We were a little disappointed that we now had to sit and wait for another four months after all this research and anticipation. We decided to pray and ask that God's will be done to find and get the right dog for our family. We agreed to pray individually, every day for a week for guidance. After that week of prayer, we decided to stop looking but wait until the fall for our puppy. Little did we know that God was working something out in the background.

As God would have it, my sister was going to a breeder out of town to buy her second dog from an Amish family. To her amazement, she saw some puppies that looked similar to what we were looking for. She asked the lady about the puppies then promptly video called us to show us what she had found. Another mix of a doodle that we had overlooked was the Irish doodle (a mix between an Irish Setter and a Poodle). Our daughter was visiting at the time, and we all immediately started to research this breed of dog while still looking at the puppies via the video call. Our son fell in love with the puppy. Though we shouldn't have been, we were surprised at how God had provided a dog for the family that met all of our needs, and the best part was, we only had to wait a week to get it! What a blessing! We got our dog the last few days in August.

In Genesis chapter 24, the story is told of Abraham's most trusted servant Eliezer who was tasked with getting a wife for his master's son Isaac. In the story, the servant prayed a very specific prayer to God for guidance. In his prayer, he asked that the perfect wife for his master's son, Isaac, offer him water to drink and water his camel. God, in His infinite love and wisdom, granted his prayer and request. God is always working in the background, even when we can not see the end result. All we have to do is pray, have faith, and trust that God will take care of every situation in our lives.

Reflection

Describe a personal situation when you ran ahead and did your own thing without waiting or thinking. What was the outcome of your actions?

_____

_____

_____

_____

_____

_____

_____

_____

_____

_____

_____

Read the text found in Psalm 27:14. What key thoughts and ideas can you infer based on this text?

_____

_____

_____

_____

_____

_____

_____

_____

_____

_____

_____

_____

Patience And Love

The puppy's first night home was a little rough. Our little bundle of joy was not accustomed to being away from his puppy brothers, sisters, and mom. Needless to say, he howled and cried for most of the night. My very excited kids comforted him and slept beside him and his playpen all night long. They catered to his every sad and crying need until he felt comfortable and went to sleep, only to awaken an hour later with more howling and yelping.

Every time he woke up, they comforted him and reassured him that everything was safe and that he was loved. They exhibited patience and love beyond measure through this challenging night. That night, they showed their love and patience for the newest member of the family. It was truly amazing to see how much attention and love they showed to this helpless and needy puppy.

In the morning, it was time to relieve them and allow them to sleep. My kids went to their beds to get their much-needed sleep. To be honest, this puppy was so adorable. I could fully understand how they would want to endure all this torture and sleeplessness. The love, patience, and care they showed through that difficult time reminded me of how we should be in our daily lives.

The Bible tells us the story of Gideon, a man chosen by God to lead the Israelite army into battle. Gideon was from the least significant family, from the least significant tribe of the Israelite nation, yet God chose him. Gideon was scared of the task and asked God to show him signs that what he was asking him was certain. In His patient and loving nature, God took the time night after night to show Gideon that He loved him and that He would be with him. The story ends with Gideon leading a tiny army of 300 soldiers into a battle against a superior army, only to be triumphant. Just as in the story of the puppy's first night home, sometimes patience and love are what is needed to get us to where God needs us to be.

Reflection

It is often difficult to exhibit patience with people when they take forever to do something that we really need. Explain a situation when you were not patient with a loved one. What was the outcome of your actions?

_____

_____

_____

_____

_____

_____

_____

_____

_____

_____

Read the text found in 1 Corinthians 13:4. Describe what you think would happen if you followed the guidelines outlined in the text you just read.

_____

_____

_____

_____

_____

_____

_____

_____

_____

_____

Forgiveness From Accidents

When you bring a puppy home for the first time, some things are just expected. For example, there will be many sleepless nights, many things will be damaged, and there will be many bathroom accidents. Our family insisted on starting the house-training process the first day we brought Xander home. We took him out to use the bathroom every hour during the day and every two hours at night. We had him confined to an area that was free of carpets and capable of being easily cleaned. After all, accidents were expected from a puppy this young.

Even when taking him out every hour during the day, he still had accidents. Most of the time, these accidents took place right after drinking water or when he went into a new area od the house. Over time, we noticed a pattern and began to adjust accordingly. Over the first week, we learned more about our puppy, his habits, and his schedule. By the end of the first week, we were tired of all those nightly bathroom breaks, but we experienced fewer and fewer accidents. The key was to be vigilant, patient, and forgiving. This was necessary since he was the equivalent of a two-year-old baby, not knowing what was right or wrong, good or bad, or how to control bodily functions.

In Genesis, the story of Abraham shows us how God works with us to guide and direct our lives. Genesis gives us the account of how God promises Abraham that he would make him a father of a great nation. Abraham, in his haste, attempts to help God in fulfilling His promise to him. In the process, Abraham makes a mess of his family life and is forced to send his son, Ishmael, and his mother Hagar, away. This act committed by Abraham was a total violation of God's trust, but God, in His love for humanity, forgave his lack of faith and restored him back to greatness.

Just like Xander and Abraham, we have all fallen short of the glory of God. We have diverted from the path that He has outlined for providing us the best opportunities of service to Him. He is forever patient, and always ready and willing to forgive us and restore us into His family. All we have to do is turn to Him and ask for forgiveness. He is even willing to meet us halfway.

Reflection

Has there ever been a time you believed that you did something that was unforgivable? Explain how you felt as a result of your thoughts and actions.

_____

_____

_____

_____

_____

_____

_____

_____

_____

_____

Read the text found in 1 John 1:9. Based on the text, what does God require from us in order to be forgiven?

_____

_____

_____

_____

_____

_____

_____

_____

_____

_____

_____

Guidance With Love

One of the first things a responsible dog owner should accomplish is to ensure that their dog knows how to walk while on a leash. When dogs can walk on a leash, it makes life better and safer for both the owner and the dog. Dogs without leash training can run into the road, attack people or other dogs, or get injured or killed by cars. It takes time to train dogs to learn how to walk and be comfortable walking on a leash.

The first step in getting our puppy trained for walking with a leash was making sure he was comfortable with a leash. It is important he understood the leash was there to help him stay safe, not take away all of his fun. Our puppy liked putting part of the leash in his mouth and pretending to walk himself. After a week of training, he walked correctly with a leash. As long as he gets his free time during the walking process, he is very content walking anywhere without tripping me up. He may not be the perfect walking companion yet, but we have a bond centered around trust for each other.

Our loving God is omniscient, which means all-knowing. Proverbs 3:5-6 states that we, as God's children, must trust in Him with all of our hearts, even when our limited understanding tells us otherwise. God wants us to be happy, and He has outlined a path for our lives that will ensure our eternal happiness. As the text suggests, if we accept His guidance, He will direct us towards the path He has for us. Like Xander, we must be willing to trust and allow Him to teach us and train us to accept His guidance. Once we understand and accept that He guides us based on His love for us, we will be able to meet our full potential.

Reflection

Can you remember a time you believed that you had life all planned out but it went a different way? Explain how it felt when it all went differently than you planned.

_____

_____

_____

_____

_____

_____

_____

_____

_____

_____

_____

Read the text found in Psalm 25:12. Based on the text and what you wrote above, how can this text help you as you move forward in your life?

_____

_____

_____

_____

_____

_____

_____

_____

_____

_____

_____

The Small Things

During the first week of getting Xander, we were a little sleep deprived. The puppy was on a two-hour bathroom schedule at night, meaning that the sleep schedule between my son and my husband was four hours for each person per night. We could not wait for when he would sleep through the night, and we could all sleep the way we were used to. Our son was returning to school the following week, so getting him sleeping through the night was a must.

The two-hour schedule worked for several nights. My son took the one, three, and five a.m. schedules, while my husband took the eleven p.m., three, and seven a.m. schedule. I witnessed my husband as he woke up in the wee hours of the morning staggering around the room as he got dressed to take Xander outside. By the third night, our son was having difficulty waking up for his three and five a.m. timeslots. One morning around five-thirty, we heard Xander crying and yelping. We both jumped up and were on the way up to get him when my husband exclaimed that he was awakened ten minutes earlier and was just laying there. Apparently, God woke him up so that he could hear the puppy crying only ten minutes later.

After we returned indoors and settled Xander back in his cage, my husband and I began to talk about what he had said. Did God really care about the dog crying and going to the bathroom? Did God care that deeply about Xander? In Matthew 6:26, the Bible states that God watches over the sparrow as it eats and goes through its daily activities. The text promises that if God takes time to worry about how birds eat, He will provide for us also. We both agreed that if God cared about an eight-week-old puppy, how much more does He care for each member of our family. We are admonished not to worry about today nor tomorrow; God is alert, aware, and in control.

Let us not forget to take the time to enjoy all that God has given to us, knowing that He is watching over us every day.

Reflection

It is easy for us to believe that God has so much to do that He doesn't have time for us? Identify a time when you believed that God was too busy to help you with life.

_____

_____

_____

_____

_____

_____

_____

_____

_____

_____

Read the text found in Luke 12:7. Based on the text, what does it say about God and the details He knows about us?

_____

_____

_____

_____

_____

_____

_____

_____

_____

_____

Relax And Enjoy The Rest

At the end of the first week of having our new puppy, Xander, we met with the veterinarian, who told us to let the dog sleep until he woke up to use the bathroom. That was music to our ears. We now wondered how long he would sleep through the night. To our surprise, the first night we let him sleep without waking him up, he slept for seven hours straight`. It was the first full night sleep everyone had for a week. It was truly amazing. We had forgotten what a full night of sleep felt like.

Sometimes in our Christian walk, we get caught up in the routines of life and forget to look at Christianity's true meaning. We are so dead-set on doing things our way or the way it's been done for generations that we begin to make our life more difficult than it should be. Matthew 23:4 speaks of how the Scribes and Pharisees established so many rules and regulations that following God became a burden. They fussed when the disciples picked corn on the Sabbath, and they fussed when Jesus healed on the Sabbath. They claimed He was in league with the Devil when He cast out devils.

What was first designed to praise and worship God, the Creator, became a chore and a burden. As in our experience with Xander, we were so caught up in making sure there were no accidents indoors, we were willing to deprive not only ourselves of sleep and happiness, but also our new puppy. When we learned to enjoy him and let nature take its course, our lives became much easier, and we enjoyed our bundle of happiness even more. Let us use our time to build a deeper personal relationship with Christ.

Reflection

Life can seem so busy that we seldom find the time to unplug from everything and just relax. Describe how you can take time every week to relax and unwind.

_____

_____

_____

_____

_____

_____

_____

_____

_____

_____

_____

Read the text found in Matthew 11:28. Based on the text, what does God promise to individuals who have difficulty in taking the time to relax and unwind?

_____

_____

_____

_____

_____

_____

_____

_____

_____

_____

_____

Training For the Future

Puppies are full of energy, emotions, and curiosity. We have to train the dog for how he will act and be in the future. While researching, we found that things that the dogs do when they are puppies are hard to correct in the future. We watched videos of large dogs sitting on their owners on the couch. The owners stated that the dog was a big teddy bear who did not realize how big and bulky they were.

From day one, we were determined to train this puppy into the perfect dog of the future. We tackled house-training from his first day with us. We made sure that he did not chew cords, did not roam around the house, or bite plants. In trying to create the perfect dog, we became exhausted in watching for all possible errors and not just enjoying the newness of having a loving, energetic, and curious dog. We had to learn to keep him busy with mind-stimulating activities that kept him out of trouble instead of looking for when he messed up. By being proactive, we avoided many of the problems that could manifest themselves in the future.

God, in His infinite wisdom, knows what we are capable of doing, achieving, and becoming, even before we do. The Bible states that before we were even born, He knew the path that He wished for us to follow. We may not always follow God's initial plan for our life, but He continues to show mercy and patience as we grow and learn to trust Him. In the book of Judges, the story of Samson shows us that even when we do not follow God's initial plan for our life, there are several different versions that can still lead to His will being done. At the end of Samson's life, he killed more Philistines on the last day than he did his entire life.

If we want God to use us, we must lean on Him and trust Him to guide us on the right pathway. We may not know or understand what we are doing on this pathway, but it is God's will, and He knows what is best for us. But, in the likelihood that we stray from His plan, He has several different options, some harder than others, that He can use to help us achieve our purpose in life. Let us learn to rely on God daily.

Reflection

Can you describe a time that you trained for a special task only to find that you were not as prepared as you thought you were? How did that make you feel?

_____

_____

_____

_____

_____

_____

_____

_____

_____

Read the text found in Matthew 24:42-43. Based on the text, what do you think about doing what ever God requires of you because He knows your future?

_____

_____

_____

_____

_____

_____

_____

_____

_____

Better Than We Were Before

When Xander first came home, he had zero house training. He was a blank canvas that needed to be designed based on our ideas and expectations. We wanted him to use the bathroom in designated areas (outside or on pee pads), and we wanted him to not pick with nor bite furniture and covers. Additionally, we wanted him to stay in the playpen actively and not freak out anytime he was left alone. Well, as expected, our new puppy did not meet any of our wants or desires at this point. It would be our job to get him to where we wanted him to be.

For the first three weeks, we worked on him learning to follow directions, using the bathroom in designated areas, not picking with furniture nor bed covers, and staying in the playpen without freaking out. Although we worked hard and consistently changed his behavior, he was not perfect yet, but he was better than before. He has fewer bathroom accidents indoors, and he doesn't pick with the furniture and covers as much. Xander still doesn't like to sleep in his playpen, nor does he want to be locked in it, but he is still better than before.

In Philippians 3:14, the Bible admonishes us to continually push towards the goal to win the prize, which is to be in Heaven with Jesus. This text suggests that being saved is a continual process that we must strive towards as Christians. As in the case of Xander, we may not be perfect yet. In fact, we may never reach perfection. However, as long as we continually work on being better versions of ourselves, we will be better than before. All God wants from us is for us to work daily to be more and more like Him.

Reflection

Describe a moment in your life when you felt bad about something that you said or did. How did this event change the way that you did things in the future?

_____
_____
_____
_____
_____
_____
_____
_____
_____
_____

Read the text found in Romans 12:1-2. Based on the text, what does God require from us in order to be found worthy and to be used by Him?

_____
_____
_____
_____
_____
_____
_____
_____
_____
_____

Walking Beside God

Xander, our Irish doodle, was not born with all of the skills needed to be a perfect walking companion. Although he had a collar when we got him at eight weeks, it was very evident that he was not trained to walk with a leash. It would take time, patience, and consistent practice to get him to an acceptable point. He went from not walking, to walking too fast, to crossing in front of me. We almost fell on numerous occasions because of his lack of training.

However, after the first week, he had made tremendous progress in walking for short periods with his leash. After not seeing him for six days, our daughter came home and commented on how well he had progressed in walking outside on a leash. We had learned the key was doing it consistently twice every day. He won't understand that learning how to walk with us could keep him protected and safe from danger. And while we want him to learn other things as he walks with us, we must remember that he is just a puppy and needs time to develop.

The same is true with us as it relates to God. In Psalms 23, we are the sheep that have to learn to rely on the Shepherd. The Master Shepherd is God, who protects us as we walk beside Him daily. The Psalm tells us that God provides our physical needs and protection as we walk beside Him. He leads us beside still waters for drinking; He protects us as we walk through difficult and dangerous times. One day, Xander will learn and understand how much easier and safer his life will be when he trusts that we have his best interest in mind. My prayer is that we learn to trust that God has our best interest in mind as He leads us from day to day.

Reflection

Has there ever been a time you were forced to blindly follow someone or believe what someone said? Explain how you felt as a result of not having control.

_____

_____

_____

_____

_____

_____

_____

_____

_____

_____

Read the text found in 2 Corinthians 5:7. Based on the text, do you believe that to build your faith in God, you have to practice using faith? Explain your answer.

_____

_____

_____

_____

_____

_____

_____

_____

_____

_____

Playpen Christians

We have experienced many firsts with Xander, our now nine-month-old puppy. One of the funniest events is how he has a love-hate relationship with his playpen. He eats food and drinks water from his playpen. He even goes into the playpen and plays in there from time to time. On some rare occasions, he has even fallen asleep within the safety of his playpen.

As long as the door of the playpen is open, he can enter and leave at will. However, if he is in the playpen and the door is closed on him, he has a major meltdown every time! He likes to fall asleep at our feet, or anywhere within sight of us, as long as it is not in the playpen. If we pick him up and place him within the playpen, he wakes up and finds his way back to our side or at our feet. He is determined to enter and leave his playpen on his terms.

I believe that is how many of us see the Christian experience and its regulations. If the playpen represents church and Christianity, we are comfortable moving back and forth as long as the door remains open. However, when people begin to put restraints on us (closing the door of freedom), we throw a fit and want to escape as soon as possible. Revelation 3:14-16 speaks about lukewarm Christians and their inevitable fate.

The problem is that like Xander and the playpen, Christians often use the church and Christianity to bring meaning to their lives. However, Christianity should also provide the needed safety for us that we are not yet aware of. The guidelines that God gives us within the Bible provide protection and security. Just like the playpen, as long as we can exist within the confines of God's requirements, we are safe from many temptations and vices that may exist outside of safety. Let us pray and ask God to help us appreciate the confines of His love and not stray from His loving arms of protection and let us not embrace being playpen Christians.

Reflection

Have you ever been in a situation that you felt something constrained you and stopped you from being your true self, only to get out and find that it was keeping you grounded and safe?

_____
_____
_____
_____
_____
_____
_____
_____
_____

Read the text found in 1 Samuel 8: 4-22. In this text, the Elders of Israel asked Samuel for a king to guide them like the nations around them. In the years that followed, it turned out to be a great mistake on their part. What lessons can be learned from this story?

_____
_____
_____
_____
_____
_____
_____
_____
_____
_____

The Right Treats

After we purchased our puppy, we wanted to start the training process right away. We went to the store to identify what treats were available for the puppy training process. We were overwhelmed by the variations of treats available in every store. There were many brands with a multitude of flavors, sizes, shapes, and textures. It wasn't easy choosing which ones our new puppy would like. Would he be partial to chicken treats, lamb treats, beef treats, fish treats, chewy treats, or hard treats? It was all just a mystery, and we would have to buy some and see which ones he preferred.

Many of the pet stores we purchased our treats from had a return policy if our puppy Xander did not like them. The return policy gave us peace of mind that allowed us to buy a wide variety of treats. So, as the training process started, we quickly realized that many of the varieties of treats we purchased would have to be returned. We could not predict the flavor, texture, size, or brand he would prefer. In the end, it was a matter of trial and error as we identified the preferences enjoyed by Xander.

We are all made differently but in the image of God. This means that He knows what is best for our happiness and our walk with him. God has taken the time and energy to know everything about every one of His people. In Luke 12:7, it indicates that God knows even the number of hairs on each of our heads. It is a beautiful feeling to know that God knows what we like, dislike, what we desire, and what we need to grow closer to Him. In His infinite wisdom, He does not require a return policy when dealing with us. He knows what we will respond to, even though we can choose for ourselves. Isn't it wonderful to know that God knows precisely everything we need to build our relationships with Him?

Reflection

Have you ever been in a situation where someone took advantage of you because they knew all of the right words to say at the right time? How did that experience make you feel about your ability to trust people?

_____

_____

_____

_____

_____

_____

_____

_____

_____

Read the text found in Philippians 4:19. This text reminds us that God will provide all of our needs. How is that different from providing all of our wants? Why is it good to know that God knows what is best for us?

_____

_____

_____

_____

_____

_____

_____

_____

_____

_____

Treats Don't Last Forever

Anyone who has ever owned a dog knows how vital some level of training is for the dog's safety and for the people that may interact with it. When trying to train an energetic and enthusiastic puppy, treats are the easiest way to focus your pet's energy and focus. Xander would be no different from other dogs who needed an abundance of treats to help the learning process. The key was finding the right treats for the occasion.

Once Xander knew that treats were involved in the process, he was more willing to participate in the learning experience. As amateur trainers, we learned that the more intense the learning requirement, the better the treats needed to be. We started with the basic commands like 'sit', 'lay-down', 'roll-over', 'come', 'stay', and 'stop'. The key was daily repetition until he would do them on command, even without treats.

Often, our Christian experience is like Xander and treats. In Mark 11:25, we are admonished to forgive those who have wronged us. That may be hard for us to accomplish the first few times we attempt to do it. In Matthew 5: 38-44, God asks us to go an extra step and suggests that we turn the other cheek, give our clothing to thieves, lend to people who may not return unto us, and love everyone that hates us. God is aware of how difficult these tasks are for us so often, he provides feelings of contentment, extra blessings, and incentives until it becomes second nature. Once we have gotten used to the process of forgiving, God can stretch us and allow us to grow in our Christian walk without requiring obvious rewards for doing so. Even though we may suffer abuse and pain down here on earth, we can look forward to our reward and blessing when we get to Heaven.

Reflection

It is easy to love God when things are going great? Has there ever been a time where you got a little upset with God when bad things happened to you? Explain.

_____
_____
_____
_____
_____
_____
_____
_____
_____
_____

Read the story of Job found in Job chapter 1. In this story Satan told God that Job only served Him because of his protection. God told Satan that he could do anything to Job except take his life. What does this story teach us?

_____
_____
_____
_____
_____
_____
_____
_____
_____
_____
_____

The Dog Smell

Dogs have a very peculiar odor that their owners have to get used to. It is part of their inherent nature to run and play outside, and as a result, they have that outdoorsy smell that honestly, just gets under my skin. There is nothing that dogs can do to avoid it.

However, some dogs smell worse than others since they are more active, love to play in water, or enjoy rolling around in mud and sand. The fact that some dogs smell worse than others has created a market that caters to disguising and covering-up their smell.

After purchasing Xander and living with him for four weeks, he had gotten to the point where I could no longer avoid his smell. The veterinarian told me that I could only have him washed once every month to prevent the risk of him getting dry, irritated skin. I had to find something to mask that smell. After weeks of research, I found a deodorant spray that could be applied to his hair. This spray would not remove the smell, but it would mask it, making it more tolerable. Being able to cover his smell made it easier for me to appreciate him.

The text found in Isaiah 64: 6 informs us that we are unclean, and there is nothing that we, as simple beings, can do to correct our uncleanness and our sinful ways. However, the story doesn't end there. 1 John 1:7 tells us that the blood of Jesus has the power to cleanse us from our smelly sinful nature and returns us into the fold of God. As in this story of Xander, the blood of Jesus covers us, cleans us, deodorizes us, and allows us to enter into the presence of God once again.

Reflection

Have you ever been in a room of people and felt that you just didn't belong there? Maybe the feelings were all in your mind. How did that experience make you feel about being in new and uncomfortable situations?

_____
_____
_____
_____
_____
_____
_____
_____
_____
_____

Read the Isaiah 41:10. What does this text tell us about being afraid and uncomfortable in new situations? What would happen in your life if you followed this text?

_____
_____
_____
_____
_____
_____
_____
_____
_____
_____
_____
_____

A Dog's Love

Every night after week two, we put our dog, Xander, to bed at 10:00. After an exhausting day of babysitting and play, we were ready for the welcomed break. It wasn't because we did not love him; we just needed the break to get other stuff done. Every night from 10:00 pm until 6:00 am, we had time to work on other things besides Xander. It was a real shame that all we ever wanted to do between those times was to sleep.

Every morning at 6:00, when we went to his cage to get him, he acted like he hadn't seen us for a lifetime. As we opened the door into the room where he slept, we could hear him wagging his tail and moving around as we walked towards him. By the time we opened the door to his cage, he leaped out into our arms and began his daily routine of kisses and love. He was so very excited to see us and greet us daily.

Every day that we are blessed with life is a blessing from God. We should rejoice and be thankful for the gift of breath every day that we are alive. God allows us to wake up and live our lives from day-to-day, and we should be willing to show Him praise. The text Luke 15:7 paints a different picture of Heaven and God, which I think is even more impressive. The text highlights that everyone in Heaven rejoices when one sinner repents and turns to God. Dogs can love with such passion and uncompromising zeal every day they see their owners. How much more does our Savior and Creator demonstrate His undying love for us every day, as we learn to love and depend on Him?

Reflection

Have you ever experienced any type of kindness or unconditional love that was superior to anything you had experienced before? Please explain how you felt about it.

_____

_____

_____

_____

_____

_____

_____

_____

_____

_____

Read the text found in John 15:13. This text signifies the extreme lengths that God will go to prove His love for us. What does this text teach us about our responsibility as a good friend here on earth?

_____

_____

_____

_____

_____

_____

_____

_____

_____

_____

Chicken Chicken Chicken!

One thing that our dog Xander loves in this world is chicken. We can get him to do anything for chicken. When we decided to train him, we used many different treats as we started the process. For those tricks and skills that we wanted him to learn, we used chicken! My daughter called it "high currency" for training. When he was tired of the regular training treats, we would pull out the chicken, and without fail, his attention and energy would return.

Xander went through a period where he would bite and nip when we tried to clean his feet after coming in from outdoors. He would nip at your fingers when removing the chain from his leash. Well, two days of training with chicken stopped all of that negative behavior. The high currency of chicken got his attention, and the job was done in no time. The problem with young puppies is that they get distracted so easily, that they sometimes need a refresher source.

Hebrews 12:4-6 states that we as Christians struggle to remain good. We often forget all that God has done for us. Like Xander, we are easily distracted from the plain truth; God loves us and trains us because He wants us to be safe and trust Him with all of our being.

Reflection

Are there any bad habits that you struggled with for a very long time? What did you have to do to overcome these bad habits? How did it feel when you overcame these bad habits in your life?

_____

_____

_____

_____

_____

_____

_____

_____

_____

_____

Read Jonah chapter 4. This chapter tells the story of how Jonah got angry after God forgave the people of Nineveh. He accused God of being long-suffering, slow to anger, and quick to forgive. What does this story tell us about how we must grow and develop in our Christian walk?

_____

_____

_____

_____

_____

_____

_____

_____

_____

_____

Always Happy To See You

Dogs have to remarkable ability to forgive and forget. Most dogs take acts of discipline differently than human beings. Even when people abuse dogs, they are willing to give any semblance of genuine kindness a chance. In the case of Xander, he would nip and bite our son on the chin and face. Everything our son tried to avert the behavior was ignored. After some time, we resorted to time out in the playpen as soon as the behavior occurred.

After about 20 minutes, our son would go to the playpen to get the puppy. To his delight, Xander was always happy to see him and be welcomed into his presence. It seemed as if Xander had forgotten why he was there and who placed him there. The excitement as the playpen door was opened was exhilarating to observe. I observed the same behavior whenever he was put in timeout by any of us as well.

Often times, we as humans take correction and discipline as a bad thing. Hebrews 12:6 states that the Lord disciplines the one He loves, and He chastises every son He receives. On our Christian walk, it seems that we must expect to be corrected by God at some point in time. God's correction should not be seen as a punishment in the negative sense but as an opportunity to refrain from certain activities and turn towards the path that God has designed especially for us. As in Xander's case, let us not hold discipline against God but turn to Him with happiness because of His unconditional love towards us.

Reflection

Can you remember a time growing up when you did not get something you really wanted because of something you had done in the past? How did that experience make you feel about the situation and about life in general?

_____

_____

_____

_____

_____

_____

_____

_____

_____

_____

Read the story of David and Bathsheba in 2 Samuel chapter 11. This story highlights the lowest point of David's governing of the Israelites. However, the Bible refers to David as a man after God's own heart. Explain how such a sinful man can be an example of godliness.

_____

_____

_____

_____

_____

_____

_____

_____

_____

_____

Loving and Loyal

I have been scared of dogs all of my life. However, I have been learning how to face my fears for the past forty days. Since we got Xander just over a month ago, he has shown me the ability dogs have to show love and affection. He has loyally greeted me each morning, with exuberance and passion. He always makes it seem like I am the most important person in the world.

At first, it was way too much excitement and attention. The jumping and the licking was so intense; it was almost too much to handle. However, over time, I realized that it was just his way to show his love and affection. I also read that not only do dogs lick to show their love and affection for us but also to mark us as theirs. Licking also calms them and releases dopamine which makes dogs calm and happy.

In Job chapter 1, the story is told of a conversation between God and Satan. In this story, God asked Satan if he noticed Job and how much he loved God. Satan replied to God that Job only loved Him because He protected him, loved him, and didn't allow anyone or anything to harm him. We know how the story ends, but the main point is that God, like Xander, protects us and watches over us. God loves us so much, and He is so loyal that He rejoices for every sinner who repents and comes to Him. He proved His matchless love for us when He sent His son to die for us. We should rejoice because we have a God that marks us as His very own and protects us every day we live.

Reflection

Are there times that you have strayed away from the guidelines that God has outlined in the Bible? Did God pull His love and protection from you right away? Explain how God shows His loyalty, even when we are undeserving, based on our actions.

_____
_____
_____
_____
_____
_____
_____
_____
_____

Read the text found in Deuteronomy 7:9. What does God promise to do for every person who loves Him and keeps His covenant?

_____
_____
_____
_____
_____
_____
_____
_____
_____
_____
_____

Playing too Rough

The training process of puppies can be a daunting but necessary task. Our dog Xander, like most puppies, loved to play. The problem was that he played a little too rough. Most of the time when he was excited, he would bark, bite, and claw. It didn't seem like he was doing it because he was upset but was always very excited to see us every day.

Since he had started puppy training a week prior, we decided to bring it up to the trainer. She told us that was how puppies showed love and affection, but we could redirect him to what behaviors were acceptable. We were informed that this would take consistency, patience, and lots of treats. We were determined to change this behavior, so we set out to tackle these negative behaviors.

After about two weeks of active training and diverting, we were enjoying Xander and his behavior even more. He was becoming more of the perfect little pup we knew he could be. He is not always perfect, but we can see him fighting to control himself. 1 Corinthians 9:27, Paul admonishes people on their Christian journey to keep their body and actions under subjection as they live for God. He states that it would be a shame to witness to others yet be lost because we failed to stay focused on God and what He has outlined for us to follow. As in Xander's case, we must not only change our ways when we follow God, but continually work daily on maintaining our godly ways.

Reflection

Can you think of a time when someone close to you was joking and playing with you and it hurt your feelings? Explain how that experience made you feel about their friendship and their love for you?

_____

_____

_____

_____

_____

_____

_____

_____

_____

_____

Read Romans chapter 14. What does this chapter say about judging and arguing with others about their walk with God? Should we be so convicted with our beliefs that we are quick to judge and 'play rough' with others?

_____

_____

_____

_____

_____

_____

_____

_____

_____

_____

_____

Forever Friendly

Some breeds of dogs are very friendly, and others are not as friendly with strangers. Owners must be mindful of which category their dog falls under and act accordingly to protect others. Our dog Xander always barked when he saw anyone close to his property, even if it was the house or yard next door. I often wondered what he would do if people came up to him.

One day a neighbor across the street saw his beautiful red curly hair and came over to have a look at him and introduce herself to him. As always, Xander barked as she came towards him, but something strange happened. As she got within ten feet of him, he stopped barking and started to wag his tail vigorously in anticipation.

Xander was all bark and no bite. He was not a guard dog; he was just diligent at telling us that someone was nearby. After that incident, we realized that it was a pattern that he would alert us whenever someone was seen, or someone was near, but he always wanted to play when they came close. He always had a way of making people, even strangers, feel special.

Christians should be friendly and loving at all times. However, human nature often takes over, and before we know what we are doing, we are barking, being unfriendly, and being skeptical at anyone we do not recognize or who is not like us. When the Holy Spirit reveals our actions and wrongdoings, we change our attitude and become more receptive to those around us, even strangers. Romans 15:7 states that we, as Christians, should always be friendly and show love towards others, as God has shown love to us. As in Xander's case, once he realized that the neighbor was not an immediate threat, he extended love and favor as he would to a friend. As we continue our Christian walk, let us remember to extend true love and friendship to everyone we encounter, and love others as God loves us.

Reflection

Do you believe that it is always easy to be friendly? How do you react when people are mean to you and treat you unfairly? What are some ways that you can show friendliness every day as you interact with people?

_____

_____

_____

_____

_____

_____

_____

_____

_____

Read Hebrews 13:2. How would you use this text to guide you on your daily Christian walk?

_____

_____

_____

_____

_____

_____

_____

_____

_____

_____

_____

Being Stubborn on My Walk

Many smart breed dogs are often hard to train because they have more of a sense of independence. In many cases, they often ignore when their owners call them because of their curiosity and thinking. For this reason, some dogs are not suggested for first-time dog owners. This is a caution that is given to let potential dog owners know that more patience, love, and attention should be given when training some breeds.

Xander is a mix of Irish setter and poodle, two smart breeds. Both dogs can learn quickly but often display stubborn behaviors when walking or asked to leave things alone. They both have the drive to please their owners and family, but sometimes, they want to walk, sniff, or explore when walking.

When Xander doesn't want to continue walking in a particular direction, he sometimes stops dead in his tracks. Other times while walking, he pulls in another direction, then proceeds to lay down in the grass. Everything stops until he is ready to move forward. On many occasions, we have tried to get him to get up and continue walking towards home, especially on days when it is raining.

Many times, we act like Xander towards God. We often reject God's wishes and guidance in our life. We often stop and divert our eyes, or feet, or thinking away from God's path of safety. In Psalm 16:11, David exclaims that God has made known the path for his life, and in the end, it will lead to everlasting life and happiness. Why are humans so often willing to turn from the course that God had designed for our life? When will we learn that God's way is the only way that leads to safety and eternal joy and happiness?

Reflection

Have you always been willing to follow God's wishes? Have you always been willing to do things that are not always comfortable to do? How did that make you feel?

_____

_____

_____

_____

_____

_____

_____

_____

_____

_____

_____

Read the story found in Numbers 21: 1-9. This story showed that the Israelites were often stubborn as they journeyed through the wilderness. How could you use this story to help you strengthen your Christian walk?

_____

_____

_____

_____

_____

_____

_____

_____

_____

_____

_____

Our Best Friend

There are so many reasons to love dogs. Dogs are loyal, friendly, loving, selfless, and forgiving. They also help us with protection, therapy, exercise, and companionship. There is such a variety of breeds, shapes, colors, and sizes that a dog is out there for every desire. No matter the reason for getting a dog, we can all agree, dogs are our best friends. After all, they come into our lives and bring us countless hours, months, and years of joy and happiness. The difference is that although they may be a big part of our lives, we are all of theirs.

There is no doubt that dogs enjoy being around us. Originally, wolves came around humans to benefit from the food scraps that were left behind. Humans loved these less aggressive wolves because they warned them and provided protection from other wild animals. Eventually, wolves and humans learned to live together and appreciate each other. In time, wolves became dogs that show excitement when they see us, show love and affection by licking us, and share their toys and snuggle up with us. In fact, apart from primates, dogs are the only other animal that looks us in the eyes to read our expressions, emotions, and desires.

We often catch Xander looking at us and assessing our mood and desire for him. When he sees us smile at him, he would often get up, walk over, and lay on our feet after licking us. In return, we rub his head and back, and he looks at us one more time before he falls asleep. In that moment, we feel the joy and affection that only a dog can bring. Humans may have many animals we use, such as cows, pigs, sheep, cats, and horses, but none show as much love, affection, and friendship as a dog.

A dog may be a person's best friend, but here is someone that loves us even more than a dog possibly can. Proverbs 18:24 tells us that there is a friend that sticks closer than a brother. God is the best friend that anyone could ever have. He has our best interest at the forefront of everything He does for us. His desire is for all of us to follow His plan and be saved. Just knowing that God can love us even more than our dogs should lead us to trust in Him and His directions more.

Reflection

Which is more important to you, to have a best friend, or to be a best friend? Explain why friendship is so important to humans for survival.

_____

_____

_____

_____

_____

_____

_____

_____

_____

_____

_____

Read the text Proverbs 18:24. Can you find two biblical examples of individuals that showed extraordinary friendship? Explain how each example showed a form of extraordinary friendship.

_____

_____

_____

_____

_____

_____

_____

_____

_____

_____

_____

More Than He Asked For

Along with my daughter, my son Siegfried Jr. had asked for a puppy for many years before we finally gave in and granted his deepest desire. We warned him that having a puppy was like having a baby that would demand lots of attention and sacrifice. The first week was very rough for him because he was very sleep-deprived as he tried to get the puppy house-trained. We felt sorry for him as he showed great sacrifice in helping house-train the newest addition to our family.

If that wasn't hard enough, summer was coming to an end, and he would be returning to school. We were in the midst of the COVID-19 pandemic, and he would be attending school virtually except for one day a week. He tried to continue a semblance of normalcy and would try to go to the gym and work out with a friend, and meet up with a few friends from time to time. Unlike before, he now had a babysitting schedule that he had to work around. He would not be able to go and come as he pleased, nor do all of the things he did before his little puppy arrived.

One day I heard my son scream out, " He is so cute it is worth all of the problems I endure." I was pleased to hear him say that since he was sleep and fun deprived for over two weeks. The text 2 Corinthians 4:8-9 tells us that Christians will endure affliction, persecution, and other negative experiences. The text goes on to admonish us that through all of our suffering, we will not be driven to despair, will not be left alone, nor suffer destruction once anchored in Christ. As in the case of Xander and Siegfried Jr., the experiences that we will endure will be worth the final outcome, a pure and unadulterated friendship and companionship with Someone that loves us unconditionally.

Reflection

It is easy to expect or demand a lot from people that we interact with. How do you react when people expect the same high standards from you?

_____

_____

_____

_____

_____

_____

_____

_____

_____

_____

Read Jeremiah 17:7-8. What do you think this text explains about the the promises and blessings of God and His promise to bless and sustain us?

_____

_____

_____

_____

_____

_____

_____

_____

_____

_____

_____

Playing Fetch

Every dog owner attempts to play fetch with their pets at some point in time. Some dogs are better with fetch than others, or so it may seem. It turns out that like everything else, some dogs need to be taught how to value the process of playing fetch, while others fall into the process more organically. One of the most problematic techniques to overcome in the training process is to let the dog see the value in sharing the ball once retrieved. According to our trainer, we just had to show Xander that fetch could be a fun bonding activity that we could both enjoy.

Teaching Xander how to play fetch took longer than expected. For one week, it seemed like he understood the process, then he just stopped. The trainer told us to have two balls when teaching fetch. We then had to make the ball in our hand seem more exciting than the ball in his mouth. When this happened, we would then throw the ball in our hand, and he would chase it and retrieve it. That worked for a while until he didn't return. We then added a high-currency treat to the process to ensure he returned, and it worked.

Once he got the gist of playing fetch, he loved it. I am not saying that the process was always perfect, but he participated in the game more often. In life, it is often difficult to find what is truly important to us. We are frequently distracted by things that seem more exciting than what we currently have, and we run off to get it. The reality is that Christians are asked by God to only run after the things of God. True Christians must search and find what nuggets of truth and wisdom He has hidden within the Bible. Acts 17:2 is part of a story that shows the apostle Paul searching the scripture and sharing the information with anyone willing to listen. As practicing Christians, we should also be willing to explore the scripture and share what we learn in our actions and how we interact with others.

Reflection

Explain how the game of fetch is similar to how we as Christians should run after the truths found within the Bible. What are three things that you have found in the Bible that have guided and directed your path?

_____
_____
_____
_____
_____
_____
_____
_____
_____

Read the text found in Matthew 28:19. This text admonishes us to go out into the world, spread the good news of salvation, then bring others back to Christ. Can you explain the similarity of this text to playing fetch?

_____
_____
_____
_____
_____
_____
_____
_____
_____
_____

Friendly Christians

Irish setters are amiable dogs, especially with their owners and family. Many of them are so friendly that they don't make good guard dogs. Poodles are often seen as friendly dogs, but due to their high intelligence, they tend to be not as friendly with strangers as the Irish setter. Xander is a first-generation mix between both breeds of dogs and is friendly but makes the family aware of strangers around.

There have been many instances where Xander has alerted us to individuals delivering packages, food, and letters. Xander has also alerted us to our neighbors' movements, cars driving by, and garbage trucks. The problem is that many individuals would take the barking as a sign that he is not friendly. However, I was alerted to his social trait one day when a delivery truck pulled up, and Xander started barking. As the gentleman got out of the truck with his package and started to approached us, Xander started to bark, but the closer he got, the more he got excited and started to wag his tail. By the time he got to us, Xander had stopped barking and was playing with him.

As Christians, we must be alert to the people around us. The Bible admonishes us to be in the world, but not of this world. We know that those in the world are different from us but worthy of our love, attention, and kindness. The Beatitudes found in Matthew 5:3-12 admonishes us to be meek, thirst after God, be merciful, and be peacemakers. On our Christian journey, we should be the light of the world - people who draw individuals closer to God. We can easily accomplish this by being friendly, loving, and kind to others. The Beatitudes is a roadmap that guides Christians into a positive experience with those who need Christ the most. Let us be like Xander and be friendly Christians. Christians should be people who bring joy to others; people who are alert, but are filled with love and passion for others.

Reflection

How would you feel if you gave your all as a friend, but did not get good friendship in return? Do you believe you could continue to give your friendship endlessly?

_____

_____

_____

_____

_____

_____

_____

_____

_____

_____

Read 1 John 4:7. How can this text be used to strengthen your friendship with everyone you interact with daily?

_____

_____

_____

_____

_____

_____

_____

_____

_____

_____

_____

_____

Always Sacrificing

Parents are supposed to have unconditional love for their kids. We spend time cleaning them, feeding them, dressing them, raising them, and doing whatever is necessary to reach adulthood safely. But we never expected that it would be the same for our new puppy Xander. We knew there would be sleepless nights, considerable financial obligation, but we never imagined the level of self-sacrifice that it would take to raise a puppy.

Since we brought Xander home almost two months ago, we have had to adjust our lives tremendously. We have not been able to travel, go out to eat, nor take leisurely drives as much without thinking about our latest addition to the family. We are no longer able to stay up late at night, nor sleep late in the morning. We now have to make babysitting arrangements before making plans to go out. It has been a tremendous change in our lives, but we love him so very much.

If you had told us previous to this experience that it would be this labor-intensive, we would have laughed in your face. There are many days where all we can say is "wow!" However, as much as we have had to sacrifice for Xander, it pales compared to the sacrifice God had to endure to save us. John 3:16 states that God's love was so strong that He gave His one and only son as a sacrifice to save us. What can be a greater sacrifice than laying down your life for someone you love? John 3:17 states that God sent His son to die for us so that we would all have an opportunity to be saved. I don't know if I would die for Xander, but I know that God would die for me, even if I were the only person on earth who ever sinned. What love! What sacrifice!

Reflection

Some people are more naturally self-sacrificing than others. However, we can all develop this trait over time. Identify a time when you sacrificed beyond what was expected of you. How did that experience feel?

_____

_____

_____

_____

_____

_____

_____

_____

_____

_____

On our Christian journey, we are admonished to turn the other cheek and love others as much as we love ourselves. What does Luke 9:24 say about self-sacrificing for others around us? Explain how this applies to you.

_____

_____

_____

_____

_____

_____

_____

_____

_____

_____

_____

The Master is Calling

One of the main reasons people train dogs is to respond positively when their name is called. In the United States alone, there were almost 5 million bites reported annually. According to the Center for Disease Control (CDC), there are approximately 2,400 dog attacks each day, 100 each hour, or once every 36 seconds. In most cases (77%), the dogs are biting an immediate family member or the owner's relative. Regardless of the case, to reduce that number, dogs need to be trained to respond to their owner's call.

Our loving dog Xander is no exception. Even though he is an amiable dog, we must always assume that he can cause harm to family and others. He is currently in behavior classes to ensure that he develops the ability to listen and responds to his master's call. Some of the strategies we are learning are the "touch" command, the "look" command, and the "respond to name" command. These three are essential, especially when he is off his leash or in imminent danger. Xander is to respond by stopping what he is doing to look at us or come to us, and sit when he hears his name being called.

Another area of concern is the fact that over 1.2 million dogs are killed by cars annually. When dogs run into the roads and do not listen to their master's command and cries of concern, there are more likely to get injured or killed by accident. No matter the reason for concern, dogs sometimes need to be protected from others.

Most dogs genuinely want to listen to their owners and please them. The problem arises when they want to have fun or are distracted by stimuli that arouse their curiosity. This is why daily training is essential when dogs are young and more open to learning new strategies and commands. Dogs that are trained can self regulate and look to their master for approval or directions.

Dogs like Xander that are driven by smell are easily distracted. This drive makes it difficult to redirect them without proper training. However, when properly trained, a bond of trust and respect causes dogs to listen to the voice of their master continually. Proverbs 3:6 admonishes Christians to listen to God and acknowledge Him so that he can effectively direct our paths. If like Xander, we continuously listen for the Master's call, we would never be led astray.

Reflection

When you were younger, did you ever hear your parents call you and you ignored them? How did you feel about the whole experience later? Did you feel guilty about it? Did you always get away with doing it?

_____

_____

_____

_____

_____

_____

_____

_____

_____

Read the text found in Revelation 3: 20. Explain how your life would change if you always listened to the voice of God when He called your name or spoke to you.

_____

_____

_____

_____

_____

_____

_____

_____

_____

_____

_____

Today is a New Day

Each new day brings a new beginning and new opportunities. Many days Xander, our very energetic Irish doodle pup , got into trouble and was placed in time-out in his playpen. He hated every moment of time-out. At first, he cried and yelped and barked while trying to climb the sides of the playpen. After several weeks of periodic time-outs, he now tolerates his punishments and time-outs without disturbing everyone.

The wonderful thing about him that regardless of how the day was before, Xander always greets us and each new day with excitement. Xander's positive attitude reminds us that we must learn not to take the previous negative life experiences and short-comings into the present and future. Each day is a new day, a new opportunity to start over and leave our mistakes behind. Things will happen; we will get hurt, talked about, stabbed in the back by friends and family, and even ostracized by others. It doesn't matter; we must learn to forgive others and forgive ourselves; the latter is often harder to do.

We often forget the number of times we had to apologize to others for our wrongdoings. When someone wrongs us, it is easy to forget that we were often in their boat. Ephesians 4:32 admonishes us to be willing to forgive each other in love. The text states that God, with His infinite mercy and love, was ready to forgive us. Even if we have difficulty remembering when we have wronged others, we should not forget that all have sinned and fallen short of God's requirements. Every time we seek God and ask him for forgiveness, He is more than willing to forgive and forget. With God, every day is a new day to live a better life for Him.

Reflection

Can you think of a time when you wronged someone and you felt nervous about calling them or reaching out to them? Did you finally reach out to them? Did they ever forgive you? If they did, how did that make you feel?

_____
_____
_____
_____
_____
_____
_____
_____
_____
_____

Read the text found in Ephesians 4:31-32. What does this text say about forgiving others as we walk with God? How would you use this text to enhance your life and your Christian journey?

_____
_____
_____
_____
_____
_____
_____
_____
_____
_____

Poisonous Fruit

Grapes, avocadoes, cherries, peaches, and plums are foods that many humans love, but dogs cannot eat. Although they may be part of our healthy diet, they have portions of them or their plants that can cause severe symptoms, complications, or even death in dogs. Their color, smell, taste, and texture may attract puppies and dogs, but in some cases, small amounts, or even multiple fruits and seeds, may lead to their death and mourning of their loss.

God instructed Adam and Eve to stay away from the tree in the center of Eden's garden. He told the new couple that the fruit of the tree should not be touched or eaten. In Genesis chapter 3, the story unfolds and paints a picture of a curious Eve talking to the serpent about what would happen if she touched or ate the fruit. The serpent took the fruit in his hand and ate of it but didn't die. This action intrigued Eve and caused her curiosity to get the better of her.

We, as Christians, are like puppies experiencing the world around us. We may not always know what is dangerous or harmful to us. All we are admonished to do is to search the scriptures and stay fully reliant on God. Eve followed her curiosity and her emotions and was led down a pathway of sin which led to a disconnect from God.

When we trust in God, He guides us and instructs us through the Holy Spirit. Psalms 23 refers to us as sheep, one of the most defenseless animals on the face of the earth. Just as we watch over Xander to ensure he does not try things that may harm him, so too, God watches over and protects us once we become wholly reliant on Him. We must always remember that when we cannot get the things that we desire or experience what we want to try in life, it may be because they are poisonous fruit, sweet to behold, but deadly when taken.

Reflection

What are some sins in your life that may seem sweet when you are doing them, but sting the soul when they are finished? Are they really worth the trouble that they cause you in the end?

_____

_____

_____

_____

_____

_____

_____

_____

_____

Read Genesis 3: 1-20. This story outlines the day that Eve took the fruit and ate from it. Although this fruit seemed wonderful to look at and touch, it turned out to be very poisonous for humanity. How could you use this story to better protect your daily Christian journey from sin?

_____

_____

_____

_____

_____

_____

_____

_____

_____

Look at the Master

Xander, like most puppies, had a tough time staying focused on anything for a long time. Being so young and inexperienced, he was always getting distracted. When taking him for walks each day, he would get distracted by leaves, insects, the leash, rabbits in the yard, and any sudden noises. It was expected of our little one, but it was becoming a safety concern, so something would have to be done.

Since we had already registered for Xander's obedience classes, it only made sense that we would address our safety concerns with the trainer. She told us that he needed to learn to look at us and respond on command. The first step would involve the repetition of a small stimulus, followed by a treat. We used a clicker to get his attention then, when he looked at us, we gave him a small piece of roasted chicken. It worked every time. Later, we would advance to calling his name and him running to us. One day, if done correctly, it could save his life.

Psalms 123:2 states that we should continually look to God, the way that a servant continually looks to his/her master. However, Deuteronomy 6:24 suggests that we should follow all of God's commands so that we will be blessed and live in Him as He commands. The only way that we can know what God has in store for us is to look to Him by searching His words daily and following His directions and commands.

Reflection

Can you think of a time when it was necessary for you to actively look at what was being shown in order for you to fully understand what was required of you? What would happen if you looked away and missed a vital step?

_____
_____
_____
_____
_____
_____
_____
_____
_____
_____

Read the text found in Isaiah 55:6-7. How would you use this text to help you outline what Christians must do to find favor and forgiveness from God?

_____
_____
_____
_____
_____
_____
_____
_____
_____
_____
_____

Stop and Stay

One of the hardest things to teach a puppy, and even older dogs, is to sit and stay. We have been working on this command for some time now. The curious nature of our dog suggests that we still have a lot of progress to make. We have no intention of losing this battle, but at times it doesn't seem easy to achieve.

We have even used the high currency of chicken treats, but the temptation seems overwhelming for Xander. My daughter has tried, and my son has tried, but sometimes, the temptation is way stronger than we can handle alone. We have implemented a series of short intervals of stop and stay. Once that short distance has been successful, we work on increasing the distance. This method of mastery and increase of time and distance seems to be the best approach.

The text in Psalm 27:14 admonishes Christians on their walk to wait on the Lord and stay strong. This command is sometimes a difficult task for us as humans and Christians to accomplish. Our sinful nature desires things of this world and sometimes makes us rush and do things on our schedule. Many of these things may not be harmful or sinful, but when we refuse to stop and stay, we do things outside of God's plan, and things may not work out in our best interest. God knows best; we should be willing to trust God and listen to His every command. Like Xander, sometimes we must deny ourselves sometimes to get a reward. Just trust that God's reward will be far superior to anything that we can imagine ourselves.

Reflection

Have you ever had to wait for something that you really wanted? Did it seem like you would die or never be the same if you didn't get that thing? Did you finally get it, and did that feeling of excitement actually last?

_____

_____

_____

_____

_____

_____

_____

_____

_____

_____

Read the text found in Psalm 34:10. How would you use this text to help you reflect on the disappointment of not getting everything that you want in your life?

_____

_____

_____

_____

_____

_____

_____

_____

_____

_____

_____

Leave It

Like babies, puppies are inquisitive and try to experience the world through their most sensitive senses. They want to feel everything, touch everything, sniff everything, and taste everything. They do not know the concept of danger, poison, harmful, or deadly yet and must be protected from themselves. As parents and owners, we have to protect the little ones in our homes from themselves.

As parents and dog owners, one of the first things that we must teach the little ones in the home is to leave items alone. Babies are told to leave magazines, knives, scissors, irons, hot pots, stoves, and dirty things alone. They do not always understand why but we, as parents, know that it is for their good. Puppies must also learn to leave a variety of things alone. They cannot play with remotes, keys, treat bags, furniture, shoes, and many other things around the house. It may look like fun to them, but they may frequently hear the phrase, "Leave it!"

Jeremiah 29:11 tells us that God has plans for each one of our lives. He has taken the time and energy to map out pathways for our lives to guide us towards Him and heaven. God's plan to save us may including pathways designed with many painful lessons and situations that we may not foresee. All that we have to do is pay attention, leave sinful things and activities alone, and happiness and contentment can be ours. However, our sinful nature is such that sin is sometimes very tempting, and we often refuse to listen to the command, "Leave it!"

Reflection

It is always easy to say, "God knows best!" But how does that saying help you when you really have your eye on something that you believe will enhance your life?

_____
_____
_____
_____
_____
_____
_____
_____
_____
_____
_____

Read the text found in Matthew 6:33. What is the main role of Christians in this world? What are we admonished to do continually? How would you use this text to justify the saying, "God knows what is best for me and my life?"

_____
_____
_____
_____
_____
_____
_____
_____
_____
_____
_____

Always Thirsty

Since Xander is half hunting dog by breed, he really enjoys exploring the outdoors, so we always made sure that he had extra time to play and enjoy nature. We quickly noticed that he seemed very thirsty upon returning from his daily walks and bathroom breaks. As soon as he returned from his walk, he ran straight into the playpen towards the food and water. It looked like he dipped his whole face into the water bowl and drank until he had his fill.

Several times a day, his water bowl had to be refilled. He never seemed to get tired of drinking water after playing and running outdoors. Strangely enough, he never seemed thirsty when he was outdoors, running, playing, and prancing like a bunny. But once back home, like clockwork, he'd run straight to his bowl to enjoy the cool refreshing water.

As Christians, we must be willing to go out and spread the great news of salvation and love. Even if we cannot be as effective as a dynamic evangelist, we still can change the lives of those we encounter every day. Matthew 5:6 admonishes us to hunger and thirst for God and His righteousness. This thirst will lead us to seek God and His goodness so that we can be rejuvenated to go out and share God's good news to everyone we encounter.

Reflection

We as humans have an internal drive that often seems to control us. When you think back on your life, what are some of the things that seem to drive you? Evaluate the impact that these things have had on your life.

_____
_____
_____
_____
_____
_____
_____
_____
_____

Read the text found in Matthew 5:6. How would you explain the meaning of this text as it relates to our human drives and desires?

_____
_____
_____
_____
_____
_____
_____
_____
_____
_____
_____

Training To Get Along

Most dogs have the drive and the desire to please their owners. They constantly look for cues and commands that direct them to what they should do and how they should act. However, sometimes excitement overtakes them and they need to be redirected to calmer behavior, especially around others.

Xander was a very playful puppy. He enjoyed being around his family every day and was always excited to see us. But it seemed like he showed a little more excitement toward my son and myself than he did toward my husband. Maybe it was because he spent the most time with him, so we were a welcome sight and change when he saw us. He would jump on us, sometimes nip at us, but it was never out of anger. He needed to be trained to greet us the right way.

In his very first class of behavior training, we explained his behavior to the trainer. In response, the trainer told us to let him know how we felt about his behavior. She instructed us that when he jumped up on us or nipped at us, we should turn around and back him. That would convey that we were not interested in that behavior. She added that when he calmed down, turn around, and reward the new behavior. What a novel concept!

Matthew 18:15-16 states that if someone offends you or sins against you, go to him and let him know what the issue is. As in the case of Xander, we should be willing to confront our brothers and sisters in Christ and not let the feelings fester and grow into contempt. How much better the church and the world would be if everyone confronted their neighbor and fellow Christians in love, as soon as we felt like we were sinned against.

Reflection

It is not human nature to get along with everyone. Since the altercation between Cain and Abel, human beings have had difficulty seeing eye-to-eye. Can you identify a time you failed to see eye-to eye with someone, even after trying your best to see things their way?

_____

_____

_____

_____

_____

_____

_____

_____

Read the text found in Romans 12:18. What is the main idea of this text? Why is it important that Christians try to follow the admonition of this text?

_____

_____

_____

_____

_____

_____

_____

_____

_____

_____

_____

Freedom with Boundaries

To truly raise a puppy with good behavior, it is necessary to establish proper human and animal interaction boundaries. Puppies are easily excitable, and sometimes, their overenthusiastic ways can cause them to bark and attack people and animals not on their property. It is an essential practice to acquaint puppies with the boundaries of their homes.

Currently, we do not have a fence that protects Xander or others from his over-enthusiastic nature. Every time a neighbor walks on the road or outside of their house, Xander barks at them. It has gotten to the point that when we take him out for his bathroom break, we quickly bring him back inside to avoid him disturbing the neighbors or the walking nearby.

Every morning as we walk Xander around our property, he becomes more and more aware of his environment, and his boundaries. This process allows him more time to become acquainted to the land around him that he is allowed to protect. He is starting to learn where he is allowed to go and where he is prohibited from going. He has developed a daily routine that shows he is beginning to understand how far he rules around him.

The story of Samson found in Judges chapter 13-16 tells of a Nazirite who was born to judge and save the Israelites in a time when they needed protection the most. God told his parents to train him to abide by certain principles. Samson was to refrain from strong drink; he could not eat any unclean foods, nor was he allowed to cut his hair. As long as he lived by these three simple rules or boundaries, his life would remain simple and easy to maneuver and understand. As in the case of Xander, knowing the boundaries of your life and sticking to them is the best way to keep your life simple and in line with the will of the Master. Any deviation from the will of the Master, God, our creator, may lead to a life of many freedoms but also a life that leads to pain and sorrows.

Reflection

Can you identify a time that you couldn't wait to be free of the restrictions of home, a job, or a situation? When you were free from that restriction, how was your life different? Were you fully free of all restrictions?

_____

_____

_____

_____

_____

_____

_____

_____

_____

_____

We can easily identify examples of people who have limited life and interpersonal boundaries. Human nature tends to want to control others to get what they want. What advice does Titus 2:12 give us about boundaries?

_____

_____

_____

_____

_____

_____

_____

_____

_____

_____

_____

Baby Steps

Puppies, like most mammals, are born not knowing how to handle the world around them. They are unable to see, hear, and smell properly until their third week of life. It is strange to imagine, but until three weeks, social interactions with siblings are minimal. However, between weeks three to eight, puppies begin to socialize with their siblings and experience the world around them. By week eight, they are weaned and able to be adopted into a new home.

Xander was adopted into our family eight weeks after he was born. He was a cute little bundle of joy and curiosity, and we were thrilled to have him. We had planned intensely for a week before he arrived to make sure he would be safe and secure in his new home. The one area that was of most concern was the steps between the first and second floor. The area where he would sleep was on the second floor on the other side of our son's bathroom. How would he get up and down the stairs daily without hurting himself?

After about two weeks of being in his new home, he entered and left the house using the three steps he had to master. The fifteen steps to get up or down to his area, however, were too much for him to master without injury. We agreed to carry him until he was able to master these steps, especially when he first woke up and when heading to bed. This plan worked until he was three and a half months old when he tried to follow our son upstairs one night. Once he made it up, we knew that he would be able to handle it with encouragement.

God has promised His people that He is forever watching over us and guiding us every step of the way. 1 Corinthians 10:13 promises that God is faithful to His people, and He will not allow us to be tempted more than we can suffer. This means that sometimes, we will have to take baby steps as we learn and mature as Christians. It also means that sometimes God picks us up and carries us through our difficult times. Other times, He lets us go through our trials and tribulations, but He is always right there beside us, every step of the way. God will never leave us nor forsake us.

Reflection

The Christian walk is a life-long journey that takes us on a very narrow path. Why are baby steps so important for a person now starting their Christian journey?

_____

_____

_____

_____

_____

_____

_____

_____

_____

_____

It is a common response for humans to compare themselves to their friends, family, and people around them. Read the text found in Matthew 7:13-14. Why do you think it is important to not look at others for Christian validation and guidance?

_____

_____

_____

_____

_____

_____

_____

_____

_____

_____

This Way

Dogs do not all experience the world in the same way. In fact, sighthounds experience the world using sight and speed in comparison to their other senses. Examples of these hounds include Greyhounds, whippets, Afghan Hound, Irish Wolfhound, and Borzoi. Sighthounds tend to have an athletic appearance with long legs, a deep chest, and a long pointed mouth. These features allow them to see their prey and catch them as quickly as possible.

The German Shorthaired Pointer, Coonhound, Labrador Retriever, German Shepherd, Beagle, Bloodhound, and Basset Hound are known for their smelling ability. Scent-hounds are dogs that hunt and experience the world using their sense of smell. These dogs have large noses and nasal cavities that allow them to take in lots of air. Dogs that use their sense of smell generally have long drooping ears to help funnel the scent to their nose as they walk.

Our dog Xander is driven by his sense of smell. Every time we take him for a walk, he stops and experiences every yard searching through the grass with his nose. He can also be seen sniffing the air around him as he leisurely lays around or walks through the house. We cannot make a sandwich, warm up food, or pull out his treats without him going crazy. His sense of smell is so heightened that it can become his worst enemy. If he smells food that he cannot get, he obsesses about it, and often he may do something that gets him in all kinds of trouble.

Dogs are different in so many ways that there is no one way to train them all. A technique that works for one dog may not work for another the same way. As Christians, we often wonder why God sends us down one pathway and other people down another. God knows our strengths and weaknesses, and He has outlined a path that leads us back to His loving arms of protection. Psalm 25: 10 tells us that God's paths for us are built from a point of love and faithfulness. With God, one way doesn't work for every Christian. We have to trust that God, in His omniscience can guide us safely through everything that life sends our way.

Reflection

Have you ever tied to go your own way, even after someone more knowledgeable gave you another way? What was your reason for doing things your way? Were you correct for going your way?

_____

_____

_____

_____

_____

_____

_____

_____

_____

We can never out-perform God, nor can we find a better pathway for our lives. In Psalm 17:6 the text states that with God's pathway, your feet will never slip in the wrong direction. What comfort does this text give you when planning to continue along your Christian journey with God?

_____

_____

_____

_____

_____

_____

_____

_____

Attracted to the Wrong Things

Puppies are always getting caught with the wrong things in their mouth. They are constantly picking with things and getting in trouble. Even though they may have many toys that were specifically purchased for them, they seem to want everyday items more. Every day, we have to watch Xander to make sure that he doesn't get into trouble and that he leaves our things alone. He is always attracted to the wrong things.

We continually have to tell him to "leave it alone". He picks with the blinds, cushions, paper towels, throw-rugs, and shoe-laces. When we see him, we ask him to "leave it" as we divert his attention to something safe for him to have. The second he thinks that our backs are turned, he finds a way to get back into trouble. Although he has not made a mess in the two months that we have had him, it seems like it will eventually happen. To avoid that dreadful day, we always supervise him and find ways to keep him engaged with his toys.

Humans have a sinful nature. We are constantly attracted to the things of this world that are wrong. Some of us gravitate to gossip, while others towards jealousy. Many of us may gravitate towards deceit, meanness, and envy. Although these sins may not be considered significant, like murder, theft, or arson, they are equal in God's eyes. James 4:17 states that anyone who knows right from wrong but fails to do it is sinning. As Christians, we are to be mindful of others and not lead them astray. If we know that something we do is hurting us or others, we are to turn away from those actions. We are to be an example to the world. Once we know what is expected, we are required to do what is right. When we know that things are not of God, we have to work hard not to be attracted to the wrong things.

Reflection

When I was a kid, I had a hard time eating my vegetables? Why do the the bad things like chocolate, candy, junk food, and soft drinks taste so good, and the good things taste so different? In life, why are the bad things so addictive and good things so hard to do?

_____

_____

_____

_____

_____

_____

_____

_____

Read the text found in James 4:7. How would you explain the meaning of this text as it relates to your ability to fight bad habits and bring your desires under control?

_____

_____

_____

_____

_____

_____

_____

_____

_____

_____

_____

Drop It

Puppies are masters at finding things to grab, bite, and chew. They often find themselves in trouble when they shred, damage, and destroy things that belong to others. Nothing around the house seems to be safe or off-limits. As dog owners, we buy toys and things to keep them occupied, but they never seem to want things that are theirs. Just like human babies, dogs want keys, food, remotes, paper, tissues, and other things that should be off-limits.

Puppies need constant supervision when out of their cages to prevent them from hurting themselves or damaging items within the house. Even when outside, puppies must be watched to make sure they do not bite, chew, or swallow things that could hurt them. For example, this year, we planted tomato plants to harvest the fruits. Some of the plants were indoors, and others were outdoors. We have had to watch Xander even more closely since tomato plants, leaves, and green tomatoes are dangerous for puppies and dogs.

This year, we lost several young rose plants that we were trying to propagate after we caught Xander biting and chewing the plants. On several occasions, we told him to drop them, but he seemed to get into them, especially every time we turned our backs. We quickly realized that we couldn't catch everything he got into every single time. We couldn't be there every time to tell him to drop it.

However, our Father in heaven is always there to comfort us and guide us in the way of righteousness. We never have to worry that God will not be there, seeing everything and showing us the best pathway for our lives. Proverbs 1: 5 informs us that if we listen to God and His guidance, we will learn what we can do, what we can have, and where we can go. God will tell us when we need to pick up good habits and when we need to identify our bad habits and drop them. All we have to do is trust God and listen to his voice.

Reflection

Have you ever struggled with dropping negative feelings, judging others, or putting yourself down? What are three bad habits you had when you were younger? Why was it important for you to drop the habits you identified?

_____

_____

_____

_____

_____

_____

_____

_____

Read the text found in Romans 6:23. How would you explain the meaning of this text as it relates to your ability to drop the bad habits and follow God's plan?

_____

_____

_____

_____

_____

_____

_____

_____

_____

_____

Wait

Puppies' curious nature means that they are always willing to push the boundaries to experience new things. Xander is no different from other puppies and must be constantly supervised and kept busy in order to stay out of trouble. Additionally, he gets over-anxious to get his way.

Xander likes playing outside, even if it is raining and wet outside and often pretends to have to use the bathroom to get outside to play. Whenever he wants to go outside, he scratches on the back door and expects to go out right away, but that is not always possible. If not let out right away, he scratches on the door then proceeds to bark to let us know that we are not moving fast enough. This is his routine, even if he has already been outside three times within the same hour.

However, since we are trying to house train him, we don't want to take the risk of trying to prove a point, only to take several steps backward in the training process. Psalm 27:14 admonishes us to wait on the Lord, be of good courage, and He will strengthen our heart. This text lets Christians know that God knows what is best for our Christian growth. Unlike us working with Xander, God already knows the outcome of all our actions. God desires that all humans be saved. Like Xander, we must learn to be patient and wait. If we learn to trust Him and wait on Him to lead us, we will live a better, more productive life.

Reflection

Do you remember a time when you were desperate to go somewhere or do something, only to have your parents or those in charge tell you to wait? Did you ever try to hurry things up or get your own way, only to get into trouble. Did you learn any life lessons from waiting?

_____

_____

_____

_____

_____

_____

_____

_____

_____

Read the text found in 2 Peter 3:9. This text suggests that when we wait on God everything works out in the best way possible. What are some ways that you can help yourself be less impatient and wait on God to work things out?

_____

_____

_____

_____

_____

_____

_____

_____

_____

Aggressive Christians

Xander is an amiable dog, especially when it comes to humans. He may bark when people are far away, but he is all love and playfulness as soon as they are close. The strange thing is that he also often barks at other dogs, especially from afar. I have seen him taunt the dog next door by barking then running to safety. I don't know if he is teasing him or if he is trying to get his attention.

When walking Xander around our neighborhood, we sometimes encounter other dogs. When Xander gets close to other dogs, he seems very aggressive as he pulls towards them. By the time they are within two feet of each other, he is all play and excitement. His level of aggressive attention and focus towards the other dog could be interpreted as aggressive behavior by the other dog owner. At first, his playful nature is masked by his behavior.

This behavior that Xander exhibits reminds me of many church members that I have encountered. Many of them seem pushy, opinionated, and set in their ways. The strange thing is that when you get to know them, they are some of the most genuine people you may ever meet. Oftentimes, they have developed this prickly exterior to protect themselves from getting used or hurt by others within the church.

Human nature often looks to others to determine if we want to be a part of a group, organization, or church. Acts 4:12 tells us that we cannot get to heaven by looking to others nor following others. A Christian's role is to accept God, spread the good news, and let our lights shine. We all have our part to play in our Christian walk. We must remember that we are all different, but we can all play a role. After all, a church where everyone is the same, is like a tree where all the parts are the same and do the same thing. We have to give everyone a chance to show their true colors. As the Bible states in Matthew chapter 7, "By their fruits, they will be identified."

Reflection

In many countries, road-rage is a common occurrence on many highways and roadways. Many individuals have lost their lives because of simple mistakes or misunderstandings. Have you ever lost control of your emotions and done something that was out of your regular nature? Explain.

_____
_____
_____
_____
_____
_____
_____

Read the text found in James 1:19. How would you explain the meaning of this text as it relates to our Christian walk and our ability to control our anger?

_____
_____
_____
_____
_____
_____
_____
_____
_____
_____
_____

The Power Of Rewards

Rule one in dog training is to ensure that you have lots of treats for rewarding your dog. The saying, "you can catch more flies with honey than with vinegar," is true with dog and puppy training. However, the most challenging thing is identifying treats that can be categorized into general treats and high currency treats. For general teaching and routine training, the regular treats are the ones of choice. When wanting to reinforce important actions or to cause them to pay more attention, high currency treats are most advantageous.

Dogs love to chew on things that are not theirs. Dogs also love to bite and run off with socks, remotes, tissue paper, magazines, and other things. When caught, they typically do not want to release these objects, so high currency treats are used. A high currency is so hypnotic to dogs that they would gladly drop items and leave them alone to get the treat.

Xander learned many tricks and lessons by using high currency treats. His breed is very nose sensitive and tends to get bored and distracted easily, but with high currency treats, he is willing to learn more, try harder to please, and go the extra mile. His high currency treat of choice is baked chicken pieces. Just smelling those treats is enough for him to listen more, try harder, and work longer to get the job done.

The more you want your dog to learn, the more treats you should use during the training process. Luke 6: 38 informs us that if we give, blessings will be returned to us. In the case of Xander, by being liberal with giving treats during training, he is encouraged to learn more, faster than usual. On our Christian journey, we face the dilemma of trusting fully in God. The truth is, God is liberal with His blessings. After all, the godly and the ungodly enjoy the rain, sunshine, love, food, and many things that God has created. His love is unmatched by any other living thing on earth. With all of the blessings and love He bestows on us, even though we are unworthy, it sure is good to know that He will never fail us.

Reflection

Do you think it is possible to follow God simply for the blessings and not for a true relationship with Him? What can you do to safeguard against following God simply for the blessings and goodness?

_____

_____

_____

_____

_____

_____

_____

_____

_____

Read the text found in Isaiah 41:10-12. How would you summarize the blessings that are promised to the true followers of God?

_____

_____

_____

_____

_____

_____

_____

_____

_____

_____

_____

Leash Control

The leash is one of the greatest inventions for taking dogs on walks and controlling energetic puppies. Growing up, we had a dog that was always kept on a leash. The one time he was not on a leash, he ran into the road and got hit by a car. A little while later, he died from his injuries. I determined that we would be cautious with Xander and make sure he was always on a leash. Things were going well. Xander was having lots of fun around his yard and in the neighborhood. We took him on walks daily, and he enjoyed all that the neighborhood had to experience. Anytime he went where he wasn't allowed to go, we were able to guide him back to the path we had for him.

In the fourth lesson of puppy behavior training, we were introduced to a new concept. The purpose of the leash was for puppy safety, not for control. We were doing it all wrong! We were caught up in controlling him with the leash, not training him in what was acceptable, and using the leash for safety reasons. The trainer told us that we were to use treats to keep him focused on walking beside us and getting him to continually look to us for guidance. What a new concept!

In life, we wonder why we can't be rich, why we can't have the perfect job, why our kids can't be academically focused, and why we can't get the house we want. 1 Corinthians 10:13 teaches us that God, in His wisdom, will not give His children temptations that they cannot overcome. Like the safety leash, we are guided by God as we move through our day and lives. He is ever watching to make sure that we will not suffer and be bombarded with things that we are not ready to face or handle. Although I cannot have everything I want, I am glad that I have everything I need.

Reflection

The Lord's prayer found in Matthew 6: 9-13 is one of the most known and memorized prayers around the world. Verse 10 of the pray asks that God's will be done on earth and in heaven. Why do many prayers ask that God's will be done versus our own will ?

_____

_____

_____

_____

_____

_____

_____

_____

_____

Read the text found in Deuteronomy 28:1-5. What are some of the promises found in this text that make it worth following God's instructions for us?

_____

_____

_____

_____

_____

_____

_____

_____

_____

_____

_____

_____

Come when called

Puppies are not born knowing their name. The simple truth is that they are not even born knowing how to speak human. It takes lots of bonding and communication for puppies to figure out what we want of them. This is why dogs spend so much time looking at their owners and the people around them. If we wish puppies to come when we call them, we have to make the process fun and rewarding at the beginning.

When we wanted Xander to respond to his name, we first had to call his name. When he responded in a way that we wanted, such as making eye contact, we marked the action with a clicker, then rewarded him. The process was repeated over and over until he was able to come when we called his name. It wasn't easy, but the lure of high currency treats made it hard for him to resist. This is the process generally used to get puppies, and even older dogs to learn new tricks.

The story of Samuel being called by God, always intrigued me because of how it happened. In 1 Samuel chapter 3, the story is painted of an obedient Samuel. Just imagine sleeping your best sleep, to be awakened three times by someone calling your name. The boy Samuel got up three times and went to the prophet Eli before he realized it was the voice of God. I Samuel 3:19 states that God spoke with Samuel and his words never fell on deaf ears. What obedience displayed by a young prophet in training. Are we that obedient to the voice of God as we go through our day? Are we always listening for His voice to guide us throughout our day?

Reflection

Each person on a christian journey is called by God. We all have a part to play as we live from day to day. Read 1 Corinthians 7:17 and explain what our role is in our day-to-day life.

_____
_____
_____
_____
_____
_____
_____
_____
_____
_____

What do you think would happen if we frequently miss opportunities to share the wonderful news of salvation and of God's goodness towards us?

_____
_____
_____
_____
_____
_____
_____
_____
_____
_____
_____
_____

Car Rides

The day we met Xander was the day we took him home. We were a little worried at first because we saw videos of him running and playing, then dropping down and resting abruptly. It seemed a little weird for him just to plop down and relax so very suddenly. It seemed like he was always plopping down and looking dead. After inquiring about it, we were told he was playing until he was exhausted and that it was typical for puppies like that.

He cried most of the way home. We had to make several stops to ensure he didn't use the bathroom in the car. The car ride home was about an hour-long, and he had a difficult time staying calm. Along the way, he threw up twice and he cried, but we finally made it home. Once we got home he was shy, but easy-going and turned out to be a bundle of joy.

The first car ride had a traumatic impact on him. After that day, he would always hate car rides. The first four weeks were hard on him since he had several veterinary appointments and training to attend. For each of those trips, he would cry all the way there and the entire way back. We tried to give him treats, but he was either too busy crying or throwing up.

After two months of car rides, he finally got to the point where he could ride in the car without crying and throwing up. There were so many fun experiences and adventures to be enjoyed if only he could endure short car rides. The Christian experience is sometimes like Xander getting used to car rides. Occasionally, we cry and get sick with the experiences that come our way. Romans 8:18 states that the present suffering is no comparison to what the Christian can enjoy later. All we must do is make it through the short period of trials and discomfort; in the end, we will enjoy an eternity of life, love, and communion in heaven.

Reflection

The Bible teaches us that when people follow the will of God, their lives are not always pleasant on earth. Many prophets and disciples were threatened, tortured, imprisoned, and killed. Explain how this Christian experience on earth is similar to a car ride?

_____

_____

_____

_____

_____

_____

_____

_____

Read the text found in Hebrews 13:14. What do you think would happen if we remembered that we are passengers simply passing through this world? How would this idea help you deal with the trials and hard times that you encountered?

_____

_____

_____

_____

_____

_____

_____

_____

_____

Getting Groomed

We have all seen pictures of show poodles and other dogs that have been groomed to show their best physical attributes. The thing is, in many cases, it took many years to get those dogs to tolerate everything they have to endure. They must tolerate the constant grooming, posing for the judges in the competitions, and allowing all of the handling and poking they have to endure.

The first time Xander got groomed, he cried and whimpered the whole time. It was expected since he was only two months old, and it was a new experience. His second time, he howled, yelped, and cried the whole time. The groomer, a friend of the family, sent us a short clip of the process, and it was kind of adorable. When he was four months old, he got his third grooming. By this time, he was a bigger puppy, and it was not as cute or adorable.

Grooming is vital for dogs and their health. During the process, they get their hair cut, their nails trimmed, and their teeth brushed. For a dog like Xander, dogs with long hair, regular grooming keeps them looking their best and in good health. Ephesians 2:10 highlights that we are the workmanship of God, prepared for His delight and His purpose. Moses spent 40 years preparing for his leadership role. David spent many years as a shepherd boy preparing for his role as king. Whatever task God has for us, know that God will equip you before it is time to face the task. Your preparation may not be what humans deem necessary, but what the God of the universe knows is needed.

Reflection

Read the text found in Luke 21:36. What does this text say about being prepared? How does this concept relate to being groomed and taken care of?

_____

_____

_____

_____

_____

_____

_____

_____

_____

_____

What do you think would happen if we refused to take care of ourselves physically, mentally, emotionally, and spiritually? Would we have the ability to resist the enemy and show ourselves worthy of being God's representative here on earth?

_____

_____

_____

_____

_____

_____

_____

_____

_____

Regular Check-Ups

The first year of a puppy's life is one of the most dangerous times. Puppies are born with a low immune system and should be kept separated from other animals. When we got Xander at eight weeks old, he got his first set of shots, puppy pack 1, which was a dewormer. At that time, he was not allowed to be around other dogs outside of his home. At 12 weeks old, he got more shots, puppy pack 2, which included dewormer and protection against ticks, and fleas. When he was 16 weeks old, he received puppy pack 3, which included more dewormer and rabies protection.

After these three checkups, Xander was now ready to be around other dogs. He had all of the required shots and protection that puppies need to survive in the world outside their homes. He could now go to dog parks and be around other dogs without significant complications. The vet told us that we were good for a year and that we did not need to return any sooner unless there was some sickness that needed to be addressed before then.

This experience with Xander reminded me of our Christian journey. When young in our Christian experience, we are very susceptible to discouragement, negative influences, picking up bad habits, or even misinterpretation of biblical truths. As Christians, we need regular spiritual checkups to safeguard us from the many attacks of the enemy. In the Bible, Saul, later known as Paul, was persecuting the new followers of Christ. He was misguided about what was right and was persistent in doing what he felt was just. On the road to Damascus, Saul had an emergency checkup that changed him into a new person. The name change became his rebirth, a shift in his misinterpretation of religion. The story of Saul's conversion found in Acts 9:1-19 shows that we can easily do wrong things in the name of religion and what feels right. We must actively seek God through the Bible so we can get regular checkups. Without God's guidance, we can easily become spiritually sick and, without the right intervention, can become spiritually dead.

Reflection

Do you think it is easy to become complacent on our Christian journey? Do we sometimes need to get a checkup from God so we know how we are doing?

_____

_____

_____

_____

_____

_____

_____

_____

_____

Read the text found in Romans 12:1-2. After reading this text, what does it say we need to do in order to be prepared to live with God?

_____

_____

_____

_____

_____

_____

_____

_____

_____

_____

_____

A Change Of Heart

I remember less than one year ago, I would be utterly perturbed to enter a store and encounter a dog in an aisle or any other part of the store. I believed that it was my right as a customer to shop without having to see or encounter a dog. My fear of dogs was so intense that I would instantly be driven to rage and anger when encountering a dog. I would fuss and wonder why I could not shop without having to be fearful.

Now, anytime we have Xander, and I need some supplies for the house or do some general shopping, I call to see if they are dog-friendly stores around. As a dog owner, I am happy to hear when the person on the other end says, "Yes, we are a dog-friendly store." Yesterday, my daughter made fun of me and how I previously fussed and complained when people had their dogs in the store.

Although I am not fully cured of my fears two months after owning a dog, I now have a change of heart. I now know how difficult it is to leave your dog at home alone. I now understand why people want or need to shop with their dogs. I know how friendly Xander is, and many people can sense how great he is also. So now, when I see dogs in the store, I no longer fuss and become angry.

On our Christian journey, we are to change how we approach and interaction with others. Everything we do should be in love and kindness. Sometimes, however, we are so caught up in our ways that we forget that others are on the same journey but at different points or along different paths. In 2 Corinthians 5: 17 we read that in Christ, we are to change our old ways and develop new traits and new perspectives. With Xander and other dogs in the store, I now have a new way of thinking that is more tolerant and accommodating. This text reminds us that as Christians, we must change to see things and the world differently. We are all God's creatures. A change of heart is not as scary as I once thought.

Reflection

The story of Noah found in Genesis gives us an account of how Noah preached for 120 years and only his family was found worthy to be saved by God. What does this story teach you about how sin can take over our heart and cause us to lose focus of what is important?

_____

_____

_____

_____

_____

_____

_____

_____

Read the story of the woman at the well found in John 4:4-42. How would you defend the idea that the woman had a change of heart once she listened to Jesus?

_____

_____

_____

_____

_____

_____

_____

_____

_____

_____

The Open Door

One of the most challenging things we have ever had to teach Xander is that every time a door is opened, he doesn't have to run through it. We have been trying to train him into understanding that he cannot run out of the front door. When it is open. The trainer told us that an open door presents a view to endless fun and excitement to dogs. Looking out of the front door and seeing all of that open space with endless possibilities for adventure drives dogs crazy.

However, open doors provide opportunities that may not always be safe. A dog has to learn that every open door or gate does not mean they have to go through. The fascination with the endless possibilities of perceived freedom that an open door or gate offers has cost many dogs their lives.

We started the training process with baby steps. We began with a bedroom door and had Xander sit in front of us with the door closed. We then opened the door slightly. If he did not get up, we used the clicker then gave him a treat. We repeated the steps as we opened the door more and more. Eventually, we moved to the back door and repeated the process. Over time, he became better at not darting through open doors. However, the lure of the front door was too great to expose him to at that time.

For Xander, the lure of an open door fuels the desire for exploration, excitement, and freedom. The problem with many open doors that life may bring is that they may not be from God. Proverbs 14:12 states that there is a way that seems right unto man, but death and destruction are the results of those decisions. As Christians, we must be sure that God is guiding us in the decisions we make. Only when God is leading us, can we be sure that an open door is not a trap specially designed by the enemy to entrap us.

Reflection

The book of Proverbs has a variety of wise counsel for anyone who is willing to seek wisdom. In Proverbs chapter 1: 7-16, there is an admonition to people who seek wise advise. What can be learned from this text?

_____
_____
_____
_____
_____
_____
_____
_____
_____
_____

There is a saying, "When one door closes, another one opens!" This seems like very wise words of optimism. What are some things that Christians should be concerned of regarding open doors?

_____
_____
_____
_____
_____
_____
_____
_____
_____
_____
_____

My First Time

Before I agreed to the family getting a dog, I told them that I would not commit to certain things because of my fear. First, I would not be feeding the dog. I would not give it water, nor take it outside for bathroom breaks or walks. Well, two months in, I have already broken all of those promises. The last one was the one that scared me the most.

Last Sunday, my husband and son agreed to take the dog out at 7:00 that morning. I woke up that morning and saw my husband still sleeping, so I listened to hear if my son would take him out. At 7:50, I couldn't take it any longer because my mind was racing. I could imagine Xander upstairs squirming and waiting to go out with his full bladder. I went up the stairs to where Xander was and unlocked his cage, picked him up, and brought him downstairs to the back door. This was my first time, and I was very nervous.

He was very excited to see me and did not bite me or jump on me. I put his leash on him and took him outside alone. Being alone was a very new experience, and I was a ball of nerves. There was no one outside to help me if he overwhelmed me, pulled away, or jumped on me. We stayed outside for about 20 minutes, and it wasn't as bad as I thought it would be.

In Genesis chapter 33, the story is told of Jacob and his fear and reluctance in meeting his brother Esau years after stealing his birthright. Jacob feared that his brother, the hunter, would kill him for what he had done to him and trembled at the thought of how the meeting would go. However, Genesis 33:4 states that Esau ran towards him, hugged him, kissed him, and cried. All this time, Jacob was worried for nothing. He allowed his life to be filled with fear, not knowing that God was working in his life behind the scene. As in Jacob and Esau's story, I was worried about an experience that God was already taking care of. Lets us strive more to live in faith and in God.

Reflection

The Bible has a plethora of texts that comfort us and reassure us that God is always with His children. What does Psalm 46: 1-3 tell us about trusting in God and not being fearful when we are God's children?

_____
_____
_____
_____
_____
_____
_____
_____
_____

Using the text above, how will you use this information to help you make it through new situations, even when you are fearful?

_____
_____
_____
_____
_____
_____
_____
_____
_____
_____
_____

Microchipped

Puppies tend to get into lots of trouble, and in many cases, they cannot help themselves. The world presents so many new experiences that it is often difficult for them to resist temptation. As with human babies, there are so many things that they can get into around the house that can hurt them. But of more significant concern is the fact that they can get out of the house and get lost. Many owners put information on their pets' collar to protect puppies and enhance the possibility that a lost puppy will be found. This information often has the name of the pet and a phone number to reach the owner. Some pet owners go further and get their pets microchipped.

A microchip is a small device injected under the skin of a pet that has the name of the animal, the name of the owners of the animal, a number where they can be reached, and pertinent medical information. This device is registered and gives additional safety to pets. If a pet is lost and brought to any ASPCA or medical facility, the information on the microchip can be accessed, and the owner can be notified.

According to the American Humane Association, over 10 million cats and dogs are lost or stolen each year. Out of that number, less than 23% of them are reunited with their owner. A microchipped pet has a better chance of being reunited with its owner.

In Luke 16:8-10, the story is told of a woman that loses one of her silver coins and does everything possible to locate it within the house. When she finally finds the lost coin, she rejoices and tells all of her friends the good news. This story highlights how God searches for His lost children when they stray from the fold.

The blood of Jesus marks us and identifies us as God's property. As with Xander and his microchip, God always knows who we are. God also goes one step further; He knows where we are and seeks us out. He desperately tries to bring us back into the fold of safety. If we are not saved, it is not because of God, but our personal choice to reject Him. Let us allow God to bring us back into the loving arms of safety.

Reflection

Do you remember a time that you lost something that was very important to you? How did you feel searching for it and not being able to find it?

_____

_____

_____

_____

_____

_____

_____

_____

_____

Read the story of the prodigal son found in Luke 15:11-32. What did the father do every day as he anticipated and hoped for his son's safe return? How does this story relate to God and His action towards us?

_____

_____

_____

_____

_____

_____

_____

_____

_____

_____

The Journey Is Not Over

It is hard to imagine that it has only been 63 days since we first welcomed Xander into our home. He has come and woven his web of curiosity, love, and excitement into our lives. Every morning, we wake up wondering how he will be today, what new things he will explore, learn, and get into. He has brought us so much joy in these few short months, but it has been a learning experience.

I have not fully overcome my fear of dogs. Sometimes Xander is a little too excited to see me in the morning, and he jumps on me and bites me playfully. I am not too fond of the rough playing that he does with me, but I am getting less afraid of dogs, especially this loving family member. I believe that he realizes that I am not as fearless as the other family member, so he is a little more gentle with me.

The training has helped him listen to the instructions we give him, which allows me to direct him to allowable behaviors. He has helped me in the process of understanding and respecting God's creatures. I spend time wondering how life is, from his perspective. I love my family, and I have learned to love the latest addition to our family also. John 13:34 admonishes us to love one another as God has loved us. We know that we are not deserving of God's love. If I can learn to love a puppy in just 63 days, is it possible for us as Christians to love the people around us, even the stranger?

Reflection

The Bible admonishes us to love our enemies and people who curse and abuse us. This goes against human nature and is difficult to do. Who do you believes benefits the most from you loving your enemies? Explain your answer in detail.

_____

_____

_____

_____

_____

_____

_____

_____

God continually loves us, even when we are not deserving of it. He also gives us grace and mercy, even though we are sinners. What do you think would happen if members of families, churches, and cities practiced extending more grace, mercy, and forgiveness?

_____

_____

_____

_____

_____

_____

_____

_____

_____